MY POEMS FOR YOU

The First Twenty-One

SHASHI SASTRY

ISBN
Hardcase 979-8-89632-372-3
Paperback 979-8-89556-961-0

To the poets, my family, and friends who have added
beauty to my life.

I don't use AI for my poems and writing.

CONTENTS

PROLOGUE

Will a wee whimsical poem do,
In place of classic prologue?
Yes! Artistic freedom says 'boo',
To the editorial frog!

Who is in the audience?
Let me feel your heart to know you.
Whether near or far poetry kins,
I think it's time our friendship grew.

Did you say you adore poetry?
With variety, rhythm, and rhyme?
Then do dive in and make merry,
I promise a jolly good time.

Ah, you can take it or leave it?
Have a read now, take its measure,
Else I know you might just forfeit,
Many an excellent pleasure.

You aver poetry's not for you?
Come then, it's time to take a chance,
Give serendipity its due,
And fall in love with its romance.

I love poetry and writing it,
Join me, my pleasure multiply,
Let's sip life's heady spirit,
Then tell me what you like and why.

The Poems

A poem in a *tercetric trimeter* of my devising, meant to be sung. Sing it aloud slow and deep, dear reader, like Amy Winehouse.

LETTING GO

Grabbed at it, said, 'stay',
But it just slipped away,
My fist closed on dismay.

I see if I'd rushed it,
I sure would have crushed it,
In my craving ruined it.

It's good I let it go,
Free to fly high and grow,
I'm wiser, now I know.

Please tell me it will keep,
Forget it, do not weep,
The price was just too steep.

I let it float on free,
Drift away gradually,
And glitter distantly.

Give it some time to change,
For nature to arrange,
A reflective new stage.

If I wait for a while,
It'll come back with a smile,
And slake my old desire.

It's good I let it go,
Free to fly high and grow,
I'm wiser, now I know.

• • •

Aloud now, don't be shy; recite it out.

THE THINGS WE DO TO BE REMEMBERED

The urge to not just disappear in time,
Makes men and women do much that's sublime.
Yet we know every outcome isn't fine,
And just as many things end in a crime.

We struggle to the poles and wheeze up peaks
Rocket into space and cross unknown seas.
We paint pictures and write bestseller books,
Create noble music and become great cooks.

We know we are our name, our name is us,
It's our sign graven into hearts and souls.
So we inscribe our gifts and sign our cards,
Scratch our initials on trees and old walls.

We play for awards, patent inventions,
Captain industries and build great mansions.
Get doctorates, raise pyramid tombs,
Donate to charities and leave heirlooms.

For freedom leaders lead revolutions,
Then turn dictators of subjugations.
For power and fame suffer damnations,
Allow genocide, decimate nations.

We can give up life for our land and people,
But cheat and get ahead without a scruple.
Draw family trees to show we're special,
For fame endure Sisyphian struggle.

With life instinct's siren call encumbered,
So many of us live lives dismembered.
Death's eternal sleep our only release,
From doing something to be remembered.

In pentameter. Please recite aloud slow as you can with the cadence — di-dum di-dum di-dum di-dum di-dum.

DODGING THE BULLETS OF ANGER AND FEAR

Whenever I see my rage arise afar,
I show it out my mind's door ajar.
I am for sure aware a lot lately,
I think, reflect, and meditate; you see.

I know what triggers my anger so well,
I elude it quickly, prevent its spell.
Whenever I unstrain, it makes me calm,
A healthy life and workouts are a balm.

From anger, I will turn my gaze to fear,
It far too often throws my mind off gear.
For worry, I query how much is real,
It helps dispel the imagined ordeal.

The straighter the path of life I do tread,
The easier it is to nix most dread.
It's thus I make myself more fit each day,
To keep pesky anger and fear at bay.

Before you start, remember you must read this poem aloud. Come on, don't be shy. You'll enjoy poems much more when recited, for they are meant to be. Okay, okay, at least murmur it *sotto voce*.

THE PLEASURE OF VINYL RECORDS AND OTHER THINGS THAT AGE

Why is music more charming on a vinyl record
Does ageing together create some mutual accord
With time come scratches and squiggles on its surface
Like creases and wrinkles on our hands and face?

Is it because it needs us to load, position, and start
Go back, turn it over and listen to the second part
Often lower the needle at a track's beginning
Does all the effort lead to mutual connecting?

Every disc develops character and personality
Each time we play it, there's subtle originality
Is it one more pleasure of hearing an LP
It's ours and unique no one can disagree?

The groove, needle and speaker are faithful fair
To sounds from drum, string, or throat through air
Our senses and minds work with waves, not digits
Prefer the unbroken sound to samples and bits.

Give me old jeans, well-worn tools, broken-in shoes
Give me houses with curtains, house plants and woods
Not for me sharp corners, hard glass and cold steel
Aren't antiseptic and soulless their feel?

What we need is something like what we are
Close to our heart and not the intellect's star
We may admire what's eternal and unchanging
But we'll never love them like things gracefully ageing.

Read the poem aloud, dear reader, and you'll find a rhythm and enjoy it more than reading it silently.

WHERE DOES IT FEEL LIKE HOME?

My eyes open in pretty Interlaken at dawn,
The hotel's been lovely, and two days gone;
It's beautiful like many places we roam,
But why do none of them feel like home?

Awaking at home is somehow different,
There's a relaxed ease and contentment;
Like belonging and connecting at birth,
Being home is like hugging the earth.

It made me wonder where's home for me,
Has it been a cantonment, town, or city?
Would I say Bangalore, Pune, or Sydney?
Locations of my birth, growth, maturity.

I may intuit the answer from the heart,
But I must also satisfy my thinking part;
For it's undeniably something to share,
What makes a spot home somewhere?

Is it just a matter of time? Is that enough?
First-generation, second, third, how long?
Is it language, food, religion, majority?
Or pull of motherland and genetic locality?

Is home acceptance of a loved one or place?
A new beginning we turn to embrace?
Taking its goodness and flaws without fuss,
and hoping it will equally cherish us?

It made me think of the plight of refugees,
Conflicted feelings of persecuted minorities;
To be home, I have the unregarded choice,
If everyone were to have it, I would rejoice!

Tell someone or gently make them feel,
You are one of us and belong, so kneel,
This land is yours to hug and kiss,
Rest your bones here in eternal bliss.

• • •

Read it aloud slowly to enjoy it best.

I WANT NO ARTIFICE

I want to create value every day,
Not just meet, text, and talk my time away.

I want to relish my work and excel,
Not spin around the career carousel.

I want friends I like or help to succeed,
Not network selfishly for career speed.

I want to listen, care, share and inspire,
Not act out some leadership doctrinaire.

I will say aye to clients when both win,
The customer's always right isn't my thing.
I want to offer things of real value,
Not push something forcibly on you.

I want to spread ideas that come to me,
Not hoard them for publishing selfishly.
I just want to naturally invent,
Not jump on the bandwagon to patent.

I want to develop through deep thinking,
Not courses meant for corporate climbing.
I want to mature and grow at my ease,
Not chase success that only recedes.

Readers shaking your head at my naiveté,
Please do not think at your labours I jest,
For you may admit you have the same goal,
In the secret happy places of your soul.

. . .

A pentametric poem in six stanzas. Recite aloud.

BE STILL, MY TURBULENT MIND

I awake, and my mind's wheel starts churning,
It spins out dreams even while I'm sleeping,
Why does my brain think so unceasingly?
What'd happen if it went still fleetingly?

Would I wilt, crumple, or cease to exist?
Is it not enough that my heart would beat?
That blood would course in vein and artery?
That there'd still be warmth in my body?

Why does my mind worry about nothing?
Think over and over 'bout the same thing?
Long for dopamine and oxytocin,
Constantly seek something exciting.

I am so fed up with my busy brain,
I want a break from the unending strain,
For what I am, I know my mind is prime,
But why should I be me all the time?

Maybe it would be good to be someone else,
A soul happy, quiet, who thinks much less.
Is anyone so—dunce or magistrate?
Or life condemns all to cogitate?

Am I doomed to think till the day I die?
Music, meditation, should these I try?
O, they're just more answers to search and find!
Will you please be still, my turbulent mind?

• • •

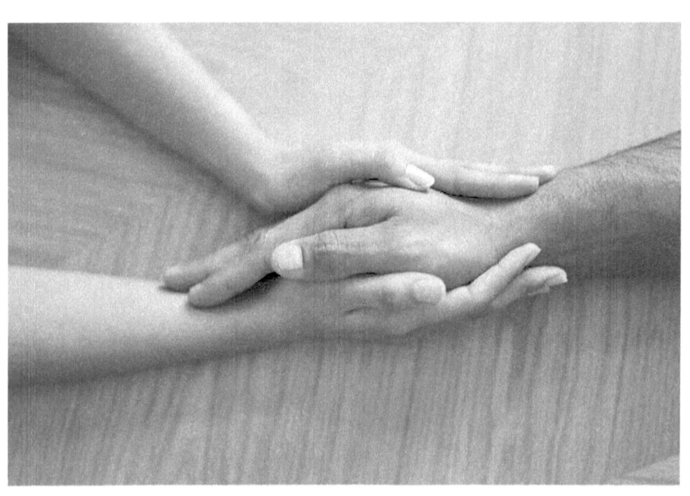

As always, best read aloud slowly.

LOVE, INTELLIGENCE, OR KINDNESS?

I surveyed my life and found it sound,
Love, intelligence, and kindness abound.
But I asked myself, and I ask thee,
Which is most precious of the three?

Love is such beautiful ecstasy,
Ancient reproductive utility,
Hard to control, often inadequate,
Seen in many animals, small and great.

Intelligence lets humans fly so high,
But it can make us quite haughty and dry.
Intellect can become sad and pensive,
It's often misused, cruel, so destructive.

Kindness accepts, forgives, is empathy,
Strong, constant, humanity's epitome.
It sees us full, is conscious choice,
Gentleness is love's intelligent voice.

Life would be dreary without love and wit,
Yet I'd survive somehow and bear it,
But of life without the third, I can't dream,
For me, kindness will always reign supreme.

In the style of a Shakespearean sonnet. Recite it aloud! Or at least listen to it with the play button in Medium. Don't just read it.

SIMPLY EXTRAORDINARY

I see how I often complicate things,
In the quagmire of thoughts, I lose the plot;
Too many options and layers and rings,
I second-guess myself into a knot.

Behold the Taj's effortless beauty,
A pyramid's unadorned impress;
The lucid strength of Relativity,
The plain force of non-violent protest.

Great people sense what to keep and what to throw,
They pare away all but the essential,
Like Jobs, Chopin, Lao Tzu, and Thoreau;
I'll make you gifts from tangled potential,
If I work out in the time left to me,
How to be simply extraordinary.

A poem in variable meter and semi-free verse. Written in the spirit of not being bound by strict convention. To be read aloud, as always.

STANDING IN THE OPEN DOOR OF A TRAIN WATCHING THE COUNTRYSIDE ROLL BY

India, ages ago.
First Class bogie,
Teen me.

Leaning against the open steel door,
Long corridor and linoleum floor.
Wind in my face, shirt flapping like a sail,
One hand gripping a vertical handrail.

No one around, myself for company,
Countryside slipping by languidly.
Train running at a fair pace, clackety-clack,
Green fields, curving track.

The far-off engine rushes confidently,
Boss of the land, planes' and ships' envy,
Emphasised with stentorian horn blare occasionally,
Mirroring the confident carefree youth in me.

Carriages undulate caterpillar-like around S bends,
The locomotive disappears and reappears fascinatingly,
Over frenetic wheels and under smoke trailing lazily.

Electric lines run alongside companionably,
Their glinting arcs falling and rising gracefully,
Kept aloft by insulators shining whitely.

Tiny scattered huts, hills, and dells,
Uninterested cows and goats with swinging bells.
Distant villagers working yards and wells.

So little for them to see.
So much to savour for me.

. . .

Read it aloud my friend, savour it slowly, come sit with me.

SUNBEAMS IN AN OLD CLOTH MILL

Left my car in a weedy cobbled lane,
By a crumbling derelict cotton mill,
It loomed cavernous coolly inviting,
In a forgotten yesteryear Bombay.

Waiting alone inside for someone late,
I sink back on a cot by the stockroom,
Haunt of the sentry who's sidled away,
Leaving nothing but relics in my care.

Many silent looms chequer the mill's floor,
Standing tall and haughty or hunkered down,
Tarped or showing gear and belt innards,
Garbed in cobwebs, dusty oil perfumed.

Distant skylights in accordion tin roof,
Beam sunshine shafts in wasted beauty,
Paths for glimmering dust to rise and fall,
To settle quietly on a world bygone.

Pigeons coo and flutter on steel girders,
Companions of melancholy old ghosts,
I too lie content on the dappled floor,
Forgotten museum with purpose no more.

I invite Adele to sing this song for us, as Amy Winehouse is no more.

While we wait for her, you must sing it aloud, in either's deep, languid voice.

DANGEROUS THINKING

Dangerous, dangerous, it's dangerous,
Thought my mind was a forever friend,
But of late, it's turned most treacherous,
Gone too far on a journey that must end.

The Thought Spirit trapped me in youth begun,
Seductive, invasive, so powerful,
Grooming me and riding my life shotgun,
Downing everything that could threaten.

With thought beside me, I worked surely,
Had many a passion and absorption,
Saw every big picture instantly,
I tasted the rewards of reflection.

Thinking made me think that Thinking was 'it',
It made the world so brilliant and bright,
Couldn't deny the good life's lamp was lit,
So proud was I of contemplating's might.

But it was dangerous, so dangerous,
Over three score years of deep pondering,
Made my heart cynical and timorous,
My head was weary, cracked, and splintering.

Beauty fled the more I understood,
X-ray vision concealed vital mystery,
Seeing too much brought more bad with the good,
Imagined many things not meant to be.

I denied temperance its golden goal,
Grew too conscious of existence,
Unwanted, wasting thoughts darkened my soul,
I forgot to smile, lost all jubilance.

Dangerous, dangerous, I'm dangerous,
If you read my works and march in my band,
Beware, my wit is pernicious,
It'll lead you to overthought's quicksand.

No! I want to save myself from sinking,
It is time to make my mind whole again,
Free from the demon spirit of musing,
I'll mute its siren song to stay more sane.

Sing, dance, laugh, and life's love recollect,
Innocence and pure nature's alloy,
Like the simple, good people I now respect,
Live with spontaneous, unbridled joy.

• • •

It felt best at thirteen syllables or fourteen with caesuras (pauses), so you have this poem in the Alexandrine meter. It's my longest yet. But nothing like venturing into new waters. I hope it flows well till the end.
Aloud, aloud, recite aloud, dear friend.

I AM MY MEMORIES

Red flowered branches slide by under a blue sky,
Mom pushing my stroller, Dad beside in suit and tie,
Daily walk in Calcutta, I was a child of four,
Say my parents, stunned at fifty I recall this yore.

I see the arcing rock that scarred me when I was nine,
The joy at twelve when my first crush had a desk near mine,
Love's hug at thirty when my wife reached Sydney,
The party full of laughter when I turned forty.

How does my mind do it, keep all this treasure for me?
Private, soothing, it's my unique identity,
I'd be no one if I were to lose my memory,
I am nothing except the sum of my history.

I live by recalling what's been happening to me,
Today writes one more page in my mind's diary,
So will tomorrow record me with much consistence,
In its etched notes, you and I find my subsistence.

Memory is survival, growth, and reproduction,
It resides in muscles, intellect, our emotion,
Keeps us whole as individuals and social bodies,
Binds our community, nation, the human species.

Love's essence is to witness and recall a life,
Commit unjudged to our mind their good times and strife,
Memory carves each of us our distinct wood grain,
Nuances of face, touch, and voice, a musical refrain.

Recollection stitches us into a family quilt,
Old photos and videos shine with time's added gilt,
When we were young, together, different, yet the same,
The fun times, the goofiness, the quirks of private fame.

We go on trips not for the moments that'll be fleeting,
But the lifetime of memories we'll be creating,
Remembrance of good times cherished over and over,
Reminiscing warmly with friends while we grow older.

We may think our mind's designed for remembering,
Yet we see it prefers forgetting to retaining,
For life is wise, keeps our mind light, a sun-dappled path,
Each beam is joyful memory, shade is hurt forgot.

Memory can be deceptive, unreliable,
We create phantoms from fantasy, pictures, words we garble,
Invent recollections, convince ourselves they're true,
Beware false memories don't end up betraying you.

We may start living too much in memory's mansion,
Cocooned in nostalgia, the real life abandon.
We get the best of memory from how we shape it,
Tomorrow is memory waiting, what'll we make it?

Our need is so strong to stay in people's memories,
We carve epitaphs on graves, churn out biographies,
Commemorate death days not to be soon forgotten,
We ensure living on through traditions begotten.

I hope you'll remember me as I was, am, will be,
Your memory is the only existence for me,
With age will come loneliness, a weak mind, much pain,
But I will be content if my memories remain.

On a special birthday, for a special someone.

WHAT WE FEEL ABOUT YOU, SHALU!

You entered our lives at times different,
By choice of nature, chance, your preferment,
We've experienced you variously,
How you enrich us, we share jointly.

Shylaja, Shylaya, Shalu, Paapu,
We would be much the poorer without you.
You are comfort, safety, happiness,
Our life is a garden with your presence.

Seed of friends' circles in Pune and Sydney,
Great gangs in AMP, Tibco, Infy, and BP.
You're care personified, friendship defined,
Drawing us in with your big heart and mind.

We sense you're classy, someone with substance,
Simple beauty at any distance,
How you're inside heightens your outer glow,
From your empathy and care, we all grow.

You of green thumb, patient plant whispering,
Intuitive cook of a range astounding,
With fine sense of harmony and colour,
You decorate, dress, do much that's stellar.

Doyen of a home uncluttered and chaste,
Friend of repair, sworn enemy of waste,
To attack a problem you're always game,
Your energy puts laziness to shame.

Health and fitness maven, champ of the new,
You never give up, always say can do.
Learning constantly, you keep growing in life,
And we get rewarded with pleasures rife.

You're at once modern and traditional,
Melding the spiritual and rational,
With honesty and duty ingrained deep,
We turn better as in your world we steep.

Loving daughter, wrote to father daily,
Gets her mother, cares for her tenderly.
Perfect form of mom and wife, we're lucky,
You're Home for Tarun, Preetika, and me.

We love you for who you are, our Shalu,
And because we feel how you love us too.
For many more decades, scores of us,
May your sunflower glow shine strong on us.

• • •

Loosely a long sonnet of thirty-four lines in iambic pentameter. To read aloud, as always.

COULDN'T CARE LESS

I was a surly baby, which is par.
My parents told of a happy childhood,
Blithe nonchalance was my youth's lodestar,
Until care crept in and settled for good.

For many years, I didn't care about care,
In its infancy, it ensured I grew.
With learning and thinking, care got more flair,
In many things, it began showing through.

I saw care's many forms and effects,
Sculptor of self, others, our world and work,
I noticed what the eye often neglects,
Care made me act more than complain and smirk.

I craved knowledge, perfect work was a must,
Looked after myself, my things and my space.
My friends and family always came first,
Care gave more joy than any other grace.

Caring felt good and care was good for me,
Yet I found life wasn't all hunky dory;
Even well-meant actions oft did poorly,
Could caring itself make life more rocky?

Concern's hot flame often burnt me and mine,
Manic panaceas can risk peace and joy.
My thoughts and the world's can't always align.
Angry caring, its goodness does destroy.

And behold, it's not just good people that care,
We have Hitler and Stalin's company!
Why, common bigots and extremists dare
Claim they, too, care; it's a sad irony.

True care is vulnerable empathy;
Without a motive shallow or crazy,
I know you only want a better me.
Someone gentler, wiser, I hope you'll see.

I'll never stop caring; it's just not me,
To care well is life's best quality.

• • •

Sing it aloud, verse and chorus!

WHAT NONSENSE!

Why are we here, to what end?
To live is such deep desire,
Why it's so, no one can tell.
Why must we struggle and strain?
For what purpose, what's the aim?

What is this life?
What nonsense!

Reach for jobs, then positions,
Grab mates to make babies,
Eat like there's a famine,
Burn the oil like a birthright,
Collect more stuff without end.

What is this life?
What nonsense!

Oh, why are we so twisted?
We smoke, take drugs, drink too much,
Some rob, steal, abuse, and cheat,
Others murder, rape, and maim.
Why must nature be so bleak?

What is this life?
What nonsense!

Can't stay faithful to a mate,
Spread our seed at any cost,
Shatter families for what?
Is the anguish worth the thrill?
Why evolve such a vile will?

What is this life?
What nonsense!

Sham intelligence invents
Deadly arms and tinsel toys,
We spread like vermin countless,
And lay our poor planet waste,
Then, rush to fix the damage.

What is this life?
What nonsense!

Fight for land, lush or barren,
Believe in gods, myths, and creeds,
Kill for them every day,
My type, our type, is the best,
Must hate everything else.

What is this life?
What nonsense!

Why's life not simply nice?
Do dumber beasts have such pains?

Are art and wit not progress?
What's great about wicked smartness?
Nothing at all, I can see.

What is this life?
What nonsense!

While we seek riches and fame,
Heart failure or accident
Snuffs out life in an instant,
Or some long malignancy
Ends our puny existence.

What is this life?
What nonsense!

Why are we here, to what end?
Who can tell me surely why,
What does the universe gain?
Can see no gods or beings reign,
There's no purpose, no aim.

Oh life,
Just nonsense!
Just nonsense…

In pentameter and mostly iambic. Recite it aloud to enjoy it best, dear reader.

SONGS OF THE SOUL: THE AMAZING ART OF POETRY

Did you read a few short lines sometime,
Of wonderful words that so thrilled your heart?
Were you smitten by their feeling or rhyme,
Wasn't it a poem, then? Did a new love start?

A poem's a string of pearls on a white page,
Grander than the sum of its tiny beads,
It shows us much beyond its little stage,
Paints a picture in the mind from its seeds.

Poems can sound as various as birdsongs,
Their melodies simple or discerned,
With each syllable just where it belongs,
They must be read aloud and performed.

Whether a limerick, ode, or sonnet,
Haiku, ballad, elegy, or free verse,
They're mind duets, and we turn and pirouette,
Glad to dance along as the poet leads us.

A thought can become many a sentence,
A line of words can form in many ways,
But its metaphor, brevity, cadence,
Makes poetry soar above prosaic essays.

Brewing poetry for a nice sensation,
Needs a deep skill for words to well ferment,
With humour, insight, imagination,
The lonely, dogged effort's worth each moment.

A poem's lines linger long in memory,
Spreading like perfumed tendrils in the mind,
Its wise, silken words line a reverie,
And lovely songs are just poems of a kind.

Poetry is civilisation's high art,
Its magic makes us laugh, wonder, or weep,
It draws us closer and softens our heart,
Lifts the downtrodden and rallies the weak.

So go write a poem, or maybe just read one,
Verse lights up life, like music and painting,
Poetry is for you, me, and everyone,
Come now, didn't you enjoy this offering?

• • •

My regular readers know I don't usually write free verse, but it felt most natural for something so close to my heart.

I hope you'll read it unhurriedly aloud, even if it's a murmur like the subject.

RAIN

Life falls from the sky,
In gentle, soothing drops,
It feels like salvation.

Like curtains on the beach,
Columns in the mountains,
Cavalcades on the plains.

I tilt up my closed eyes,
Receive you with open arms,
Peace envelopes me.

Rivulets on windowpanes,
Naughty drenches by shelter trees,
Beads on tips of umbrella spines.

Moisturised cool breezes,
Rejuvenating scent of grateful earth,
Gurgles of a million hurrying streams.

Rain, ancient miracle,
Unwitting creator of life,
Destined to last long after us.

Come, bathe the air, green the earth,
Make me alive once more,
Before I dissolve back into you.

In pentameter, primarily iambic. Read aloud for the true pleasure of poetry.

FACES

I met someone after ages yesterday,
Bare facts had, in time, long faded away,
Name, voice, and history were all a haze,
But ah, I knew I surely knew that face.

Life and genes equally shape our visage,
Prints or dental X-rays aren't our image,
Our skull's nimble cover of muscle and skin,
Conjures like magic the person within.

Which forehead or eyes, mouth or chin,
What sort of skin or teeth, cheekbones or grin,
Make a Monroe, Hepburn, Pitt, or Clooney?
Who is handsome? What is beauty?

Sensual mobile lips are unmissable,
As objects of desire so kissable,
But it's clearly eyes that loudest speak,
All of ours are the same, yet each is so unique!

Why do some eyes shine, others seem dead,
Through lovers' locked eyes, so much is said,
Is it physics or our souls' chemistry,
Oh, what a delectable mystery!

Beard and turban old aids for men manly,
Rouge, paint, trinkets for girls to be lovely,
But plastic and Botox, is it wise?
Leave off self-loathing; you can smile and rise.

We're born face-readers, see at a glance,
Who's shifty, trusty, friendly, worth a chance,
Steal gazes at someone tempting in the crowd,
To catch being looked at makes us smugly proud.

Our facade shapes us, but we sculpt it, too,
As we grow inside, it reveals us true,
Buddha's peace, Gandhi's love, Mandela's grit,
In their countenance, we see their spirit.

Once our faces told of our nation and tribe,
To modern life and migration ascribe,
Why features now come in such rich array,
Your face contains a world; what does it say?

. . .

In free verse, and it must be read aloud, dear reader.

LIVING LARGE

I feel largest in life in those occasional interludes,
In which an instant in time seems like an eternity,
And the moment has limitless possibilities I can influence,
Marked by the giant hand of the clock of infinity.
The world is lit by a blindingly clear light,
That falls out of the bluest of skies and whitest of clouds,
Onto me and the objects around me.
A cool zephyr ripples over my warming skin,
The concrete grains of a wall under my hand,
The sheen of metal and the blades of green grass,
Everything stilled in a crystalline sharpness,
And a word, gesture or smile from me,
Diffuses benevolence and something good over the world.
Then, the unhurried sliding forward of the red hand,
Of the giant white clock standing aslant over the world,
And the next infinite exalted moment.
A state of flow, of grace.
I think this is what living large is.
Not money, not power, nor title, nor sex,
Nor being without a care about anything or anyone,
But being good enough at something I love,
To leave a little eddy of beauty and peace somewhere,
Noticed by me, even if by no one else.

In free verse, best read aloud to enjoy it fully, dear friend.

OVER THE EDGE

Over the edge
I step tentatively,
into the unknown
terrain of my mind.
The flowers of the valley
lift their bright faces,
and smile up at me,
Their scent calls
my seeking mind,
The green grass beds
beckon my hesitant soul,
As I float between
their welcoming carpet,
And letting the past go.

EPILOGUE

I hope you enjoyed the poems.

I would be delighted to hear your feelings about them and their subjects.

You can share your thoughts on my website, https://quality-thinking.net, which has all my poems or on Medium at shashisastry.medium.com.

You can also write to me at ssastry1111@gmail.com.

ACKNOWLEDGEMENTS

My love for poetry has been deeply shaped by a handful of poets who continue to inspire me. Emily Dickinson, Robert Frost, William Wordsworth, W.B. Yeats, and the soulful ghazal poets of India—each has left an indelible mark on my heart and words.

I am also profoundly grateful to Medium for giving me a platform and a vibrant audience to share my poems.

ABOUT THE AUTHOR

Shashidhar Sastry—known as Shashi to his readers—is a prolific writer whose insightful work graces Medium and various other platforms.

With four books under his belt, Shashi's curiosity and passion for knowledge seem limitless. As an avid reader, he delves deeply into philosophy, Western classical music, history, and languages.

And if you're drawn to the wit of Oscar Wilde, the depth of Graham Greene, or the sharp humor of Kingsley Amis, you're sure to find a kindred spirit in Shashi.

Professionally, Shashi began his career with over a decade as an engineer before transitioning into IT, where he spent a fulfilling 25 years at IBM as an enterprise architect.

An Indian Australian, Shashi spent many years in Sydney with his family, who are now happily settled between Sydney and Pune.

Discover Shashi's books, essays, and poetry at:

quality-thinking.net

shashisastry.medium.com

www.facebook(instagram).com/ShashiSastry1111/

shashisastry.substack.com

IMAGE CREDITS

All images used were classified as free for reuse or created by me in Canva Pro. In case of any inadvertent incorrect usage, please get in touch with the author at ssastry1111@gmail.com for prompt action.

Au revoir!